WILD BIRD GUIDES

Tufted Titmouse

WILD BIRD GUIDES

Tufted Titmouse

Thomas C. Grubb, Jr.

STACKPOLE BOOKS

Published by
STACKPOLE BOOKS
5067 Ritter Road
Mechanicsburg, PA 17055

Printed in Hong Kong

10 9 8 7 6 5 4 3 2 1

First edition

Cover design by Tracy Patterson

Cover photo by Richard Day/Daybreak Imagery

Library of Congress Cataloging-in-Publication

Grubb, Thomas C.
    Tufted titmouse / Thomas C. Grubb, Jr.—1st ed.
       p. cm.—(Wild bird guides)
    Includes bibliographical references.
    ISBN 0-8117-2967-2
    1. Tufted titmouse. 2. Black-crested titmouse. I. Title.
  II. Series
    QL696.P215G78   1998
    598.8'24—dc21   97-18000
                                                       CIP

For Jill

Acknowledgments

Over the years, many students and colleagues have worked with me on research projects involving titmice, and many landowners have granted us permission to conduct field projects on their property. I thank all of these students, friends, and neighbors for their help and interest, and my family for their continuing support.

Contents

Introduction

This book is divided into three parts. "What Titmice Are" (chapters 1 and 2) examines some of the distinguishing characteristics of titmice. "What Titmice Do" (chapters 3 and 4) explores how such features play a role in the natural history of titmice. Finally, "What Titmice Mean" (chapter 5) considers why titmice are important parts of our surroundings, both as indicators of environmental health and as elevators of our spirits.

Introducing Tufted and Black-crested Titmice

At first glance, the Tufted and Black-crested Titmice appear to be small, rather nondescript woodland birds. Ah, but how interesting they are, and what they can teach us! Both weigh about 20 grams, a rather typical size for a songbird and just about the same weight as a mammalian mouse. Both are gray above and whitish below. The outstanding difference between the two forms concerns the color of the crest. The crest of the Tufted Titmouse is the same color as the plumage on the sides and back of the head; the Black-crested Titmouse, as its name implies, has a coal-black crest that contrasts strongly with the gray of the head and back. Both titmice are bouncy, sometimes saucy in manner, and even from a great distance they can be heard calling and scolding as they forage in social groups for their food of insects and seeds. The Tufted Titmouse is a resident of eastern North America, and the Black-crested Titmouse occurs in Oklahoma, Texas, and down into Mexico. The two forms meet along a narrow band running along the eastern edge of the Edwards Plateau in Texas.

Now officially considered to be two subspecies of one species, namely the Tufted Titmouse, the two forms were held to be two distinct species until 1983, when the American Ornithologists' Union (AOU), the official body charged with maintaining the taxonomy of North American birds, lumped them together into one species. Biochemical evidence reported since 1983 has not resolved the issue. Based on analyses of the structure of proteins, Michael Braun and his coworkers concluded that Black-crested and Tufted Titmice were no less different than some clearly recognized pairs of species. Based on assumptions about the rate of accumulation of mutations, they surmised that the two titmice had become isolated about a quarter of a million years ago. However, Frank Gill and colleagues compared the fine structure of mitochondrial DNA in the two forms and found that it differed no more than in some other species with large geographical ranges.

One suggestion to account for this disparity of results is that the two titmice did split hundreds of thousands of years ago, but have recently expanded their ranges so that they have come into contact again. The idea is that these species are related closely enough to hybridize if given the opportunity, and that such hybridization allows a small amount of mixing of DNA to occur in the border region. At any rate, experts are still divided over the issue. For example, in 1990, seven years after the AOU lumped the two titmice together into one species, Charles Sibley and Burt Monroe, two authorities in avian systematics, treated the Tufted and Black-crested Titmice (shown here) as separate species. It seems possible that they might soon be resplit into two species, for reasons that will be discussed below. They will be treated in this book as though they are separate forms, whether subspecies or species.

The Tufted Titmouse (top photo) is the largest member of the family Paridae, the chickadees and titmice, in North America. The Tufted and Black-crested Titmice are placed with two other species, the Oak Titmouse and the Juniper Titmouse, in genus *Baeolophus.* Such a classi-fication indicates that the four titmice are rather similar and, together, are somewhat distantly related to the chickadees. The Oak and Juniper Titmice are found in the southwestern and western United States, the Juniper Titmouse east of, and the Oak Titmouse west of the High Sierra with a small area of hybridization on the Modoc Plateau of northern California. These two western titmice were officially created in 1997 by splitting the former Plain Titmouse (bottom photo) into two species. Depending on what system you follow, the titmice and chickadees comprise about fifty-five species worldwide and are found in North America, Europe, Asia, and Africa. Whereas some parids, such as the Great Titmouse of Eurasia, are exceedingly well studied, little or nothing is known about the biology of others, partic-ularly those in interior Asia and Africa.

This book will concentrate on the two eastern forms, the Tufted Titmouse and the Black-crested Titmouse, which is shown here with its wings and tail spread prior to landing. Titmice are among only a handful of crested species in North America. In its adult plumage, the Tufted Titmouse is a deep leaden gray on the upper surface, including the crest, with the feather edges tinged with olive or olive brown. Such feathers become completely gray by spring due to feather wear over the winter months.

When newly molted, the flight feathers of the wing (the remiges) and tail (the rectrices) are gray tinged with a faint greenish wash. The forehead is marked by a black patch, or badge, that may grade to dark brown at the margins. Some authorities claim that the sexes of Tufted Titmice can be distinguished because the forehead badge of the female is somewhat smaller and browner overall than that of the male. Other than this possible difference, the sexes are identical in appearance. Adult Tufted Titmice are white or creamy white along the side of the face and on the belly. There are several small, black feathers just along the upper margin of the eye that can give the impression that the birds are wearing mascara.

Birds' eyes are marked by a nictitating membrane, a thin, transparent or translucent "third eyelid" that sweeps across the eye from front to back. It may aid in preventing desiccation or, as in the case of this young Titmouse being fed by its sharp-billed parent, protect the eye against dirt particles and physical damage.

The feathers on the flanks of a titmouse are washed with rusty brown. Unlike some birds that alternate between nonbreeding and breeding plumage, Tufted Titmice remain the same color year-round.

The Black-crested Titmouse resembles its tufted relative very closely in all aspects of plumage except the forehead and crest. The black-crested form has a white forehead patch and black crest, whereas the tufted form has a black forehead and gray crest. Where the two forms interbreed in Texas, intermediates occur in which the crest varies from a gray color only slightly darker than the body plumage to somewhat brownish.

Recently fledged young, such as this young Tufted Titmouse not long out of the nest, retain what is called the juvenile plumage until late summer or early autumn, when they molt all the body plumage and some or all of the flight feathers, thus coming to resemble their elders rather closely. The juvenile plumage is light gray above and dull whitish gray below, with the flanks only faintly tinged with pinkish brown. The crest is not distinct in juveniles, and the forehead badge is more brownish gray than black. Overall, the juvenile plumage seems more loosely knit than that of adults, as indeed it is. The very small barbules that link together the barbs of a feather in Velcrolike fashion are many fewer in number on the feathers of juveniles.

The adult bill is quite blue-black, and the legs and feet are steel gray. During their first months out of the nest, juveniles have brownish black bills, and the gray of their legs and feet has a pinkish tinge as if not yet fully pigmented.

Ecologists are interested in knowing how survivorship, the term applied to the proportion of animals surviving some period of time, varies with the animals' age. Survivorship values are part of the information needed to calculate whether a population is increasing or decreasing in number and, therefore, its chances of extinction. For such calculations to be valid, the survivorship of birds of different ages must be known. This can present a problem in birds such as titmice, because after they have finished their autumn, or prebasic, molt, the young of the year come to resemble the adults almost exactly.

Through the years, bird banders have developed several techniques that are useful in classifying such birds as either young of the year or adult. The most important technique is called "skulling." Birds hatch with just a single layer of skull. During their first autumn of life, the skull, or cranium, gradually divides into two layers separated by a space. This process has been termed pneumatization. After pneumatization is complete, the two layers are connected by a series of strutlike bony extensions.

Ornithologists have discovered that by moistening and then moving apart the feathers of the crown, they can view the skull through the nearly transparent skin. If the skull appears pink, the two layers of the cranium have not yet become separated, and the bird may be classified as a young of the year. If the skull is dullish white in color, pneumatization has been completed, and the age of the bird is not clear. It may be an adult or it may be a young-of-the-year bird that has already completed cranial separation.

Titmice do not complete pneumatization until very late in their first autumn or early winter. Carolina Chickadees in Ohio, where I live, have finished skull pneumatization by November, so any unbanded birds we catch thereafter through the winter must be classed as age unknown. Our Tufted Titmice do not complete pneumatization until considerably later, and quite often we can still find birds with pink skulls in January, allowing us to age them as young-of-the-year birds even at that late date.

Another way to age titmice has to do with the molt. Young titmice drop and replace all nine primaries, or outermost wing feathers, on each wing in their first autumn, but many do not molt the feathers that cover the base of the primaries on the upper surface of the wing, called the primary coverts. So if a bird caught from October on has old, brownish, worn primary coverts, we know it is a young bird. Some young birds do molt these feathers, so if a titmouse caught from autumn on has new primary coverts, it cannot be assigned to an age category. Once a titmouse has reached adulthood, there is no known way to tell its age.

The range of the Tufted Titmouse extends down the Atlantic coast, from middle New England as far as southern Florida. It is found along the Gulf coast to eastern Texas, where its range turns north and follows the eastern margin of the Great Plains as far as southeastern Minnesota and southwestern Wisconsin. The species' northern boundary extends eastward through Michigan, southern Ontario, and northern New York to New England.

Only a few decades ago, it was unheard of to find titmice in northern coniferous forests. Historically, the species has been a year-round resident of eastern deciduous woodlands, and it still reaches the greatest densities in locations such as the Ohio Valley, where it has access to abundant acorn or beech mast crops during the winter. Now, however, the species range surrounds Lake Erie and is pushing north into Maine, Michigan, and Wisconsin. This very likely is due to the vast increase in the winter feeding of birds. Now titmice can survive the winter on the artificial "mast supply" of sunflower seeds in areas with no natural mast-producing trees and with heavy snow cover that would prevent titmice from finding fallen mast even if it were there. Indeed, titmice cache such seeds extensively, just as they would acorns or beechnuts. Food caching is a very important adaptation for winter survival. Tufted Titmice are found throughout the South and East, except for extreme southeast Florida, another area beyond the range of oak and beech trees. I wonder if titmice would extend their range into southeast Florida if residents there put out sunflower seeds?

The Black-crested Titmouse takes up where the Tufted Titmouse leaves off in extreme southern Oklahoma and eastern Texas. The range extends southward along the eastern rim of the Edwards Plateau and on into Mexico beyond the Rio Grande Valley to central Coahuila, Hidalgo, Veracruz, and easternmost Chihuahua. The western edge of the range extends north through the mountains of southwest Texas, then diagonally across the southern Texas panhandle to Oklahoma. The Black-crested Titmouse is most common in dry mesquite-shrub habitat. The western edge of its range seems limited by moisture requirements; along that boundary, it is confined to canyons and corridors of cottonwoods along streams.

The question of whether the Tufted and Black-crested Titmice are one species or two is quite interesting, not just because it affects birders' life lists, but also because it represents a current point of uncertainty in science. According to the prevailing biological definition, a species is made up of actually or potentially interbreeding populations that are reproductively separated from other such populations. So what are we to make of animals that appear to be hybrids between two assumed species? This fledgling appears to be a hybrid of Tufted and Black-crested Titmice.

Here's the situation. The range of the Tufted Titmouse extends westward into the drier and drier country of Texas and Oklahoma. It meets the range of the Black-crested Titmouse along certain narrow fronts, such as the border of the Edwards Plateau, shown at right, where there appears to be a sharp environmental gradient in moisture. The tufted is on the moister side and the black-crested on the drier side. Where the breeding ranges come together along this front, usually along riverside woodlands that traverse the boundary between the two ranges, titmice occur that are midway in appearance between the two forms. Such hybrids are marked by intermediate forehead colors and by crest colors that run to dark gray rather than to either tufted gray or crested black.

Reproductive isolation between two species does not mean that they do not interbreed, only that they are reproductively isolated. The isolation could occur after fertilization if the hybrid young are inviable or infertile. We have very clear evidence for the viability of hybrids, but little or no knowledge of their fertility and whether the offspring of hybrids are also fertile.

This question of the fertility of offspring is crucial. According to one group of experts, there are really two species, and the hybrid zone occurs because of mating "mistakes" made by birds of the parental species. Although hybrids are produced, they have low fertility, so the hybrid characteristics do not spread back into the two parent populations. The opposing view maintains that there is really only one species that straddles a steep environmental gradient (probably moisture) along the Edwards Plateau, and it just happens that birds that appear to be hybrids are best adapted to survive and reproduce at one point along the gradient.

To find out which explanation is correct, we need to determine the reproductive success of the hybrids. If they are not fertile, as might be indicated, for example, by hatching failure of a clutch in a nestbox, or if their offspring are not fertile, then we might conclude that the two titmice really are different species because they are reproductively isolated from each other. But if the hybrids are as fertile in their part of the moisture gradient as either parental form is in its part of the gradient, we might conclude that we are dealing with only one species. As I write, the answer is not in, but the necessary fieldwork has been started.

The Black-crested Titmouse is lighter in weight than the Tufted Titmouse. The lower weight is thought to be advantageous in hot climates such as that of Texas because it increases the surface-to-volume ratio, promoting the dissipation of metabolic heat. Currently, we have no information on whether hybrids are intermediate between the two parental forms in physiological processes as well as in appearance and body mass.

2

Behavior and Communication

Except for a few dozen species that during the course of evolution have lost the ability to fly, birds are flying machines that require considerable time devoted to care and maintenance. Such plumage care suffers when other activities assume higher priority. Periodically in my studies, I capture for banding a titmouse, usually a young-of-the-year bird, that apparently has not been washing and preening its feathers. It seems likely that these birds are having such difficulty finding sufficient food that they are forced to forgo the normal preening. During warm weather, titmice routinely bathe at least once a day.

Titmice seem to be aware that they are extremely vulnerable to predation while bathing and are quite wary as they approach the water. Although I have seen a wintering Tufted Titmouse apparently attempting to bathe in snow, bathing seems to be abandoned in northern latitudes during the winter when there is no standing water.

After its bath, a titmouse flies to a sheltered location and shakes the water from its plumage.

Following bathing and shaking, and at other times when time permits, titmice undertake meticulous cleaning and reordering of their plumage. The flight feathers are drawn individually through the bill to reconnect all the small hooks, or barbules, for maximum resistance to airflow during flight. Also during preening, the bird squeezes small amounts of oily liquid from an organ called the uropygial gland, located on the upper surface of its tail. Such oil is then transferred via the bill to the feathers and functions in maintaining suppleness of the plumage; this is analogous to oiling one's leather shoes periodically. I have often seen titmice preening during the midday hours of a sunny winter's day, but always in a grapevine tangle or the like where they would be concealed from hawks. When the winter weather turns cold and windy, however, preening is abandoned in favor of looking for food every waking minute.

Where water is available, titmice can be seen drinking periodically throughout the day, and they quite readily eat snow during the winter. It is unclear how reliant titmice are on snow or standing water. Here in Ohio, I am currently studying Tufted Titmice that spend the winter entirely confined to small, isolated woodlots that apparently lack any source of water. We do know that on the western edge of its range, the Black-crested Titmouse is found mainly along watercourses. However, it appears the birds in my woodlots are getting all the moisture they require from their insect prey, which suggests that the Black-crested Titmouse range may be limited more by the abundance of insects than by water directly.

Titmice have excellent eyesight, acute hearing, but only a rudimentary sense of smell. They are quite able to spot a flying hawk at a great distance and often alert a human observer to the hawk's location. The range of pitches in their calls and sounds suggests that they can hear sounds well above 10,000 hertz (or cycles per second) in frequency. In comparison, humans can hear frequencies ranging from about 200 to about 12,000 hertz. In some birds, such as Turkey Vultures, which have quite an operational sense of smell, the part of the brain associated with the reception and processing of signals from olfactory tissue in the nasal passages is well developed. No experimental work has been performed on the physiology  of odor detection in the titmouse, but the part of its brain associated with olfactory reception is extremely undeveloped, suggesting that its olfactory prowess is rudimentary at best.

As might be predicted from knowledge of their sensory systems, the communication system of titmice is based on visual and auditory signals. The crest is basically a semaphore signal indicating a bird's level of excitement or of aggressiveness associated with dominance. An excited or aggressive bird raises its crest; a passive or subordinate individual depresses the crest until it almost disappears against the bird's crown. This difference can be readily observed near bird feeders. A raised crest indicates a socially dominant titmouse that moves directly, even confidently, to the food source. A bird with a lowered crest will hang back and defer to dominants. Often such subordinate, low-crest birds are young of the year or have trespassed across territory boundaries to get to a feeder.

This subordinate titmouse is feeding on a small food item it has found on the surface of a branch. The most subordinate birds in social groups of titmice tend to be young-of-the-year females. Such birds tend to be smaller than adults, with shorter wings and tail, and they often occur on the flock periphery only. Subordinate birds often lose food items they have found to an onrushing dominant flockmate, which may explain their reluctance to integrate more fully into the flock structure.

Titmice live in woodlands, habitats where visual signals are readily interrupted. Thus, it is not surprising that they have no long-distance visual communication patterns, such as the aerial courtship displays of open-country Horned Larks. Instead, they communicate with visual displays only over short distances, on the order of several meters, and rely on a varied vocal repertoire for longer-distance communication.

The longest-distance vocal signal used routinely is the song, which is usually employed by males. The song is usually a series of whistled notes, perhaps best rendered as *peter-peter-peter,* with the second note of each *peter* given at a lower pitch than the first note. Sometimes up to ten or a dozen songs are given in quick succession. Some birds are so persistent in this song that it takes on the background quality of locust song as one walks through the early-spring woods. Singing rate can vary from one to two songs a minute to as many as thirty-five songs a minute. Why is this? Some researchers have suggested that a high-quality male in good nutritional condition can afford to sing more, and look for food less, than a male in poorer condition, and that females assess the quality of prospective mates by the rate of their singing.

Some students of Tufted Titmouse song have identified as many as twenty recognizably different variations of the basic *peter-peter* song type—recognizably different, that is, to humans. It is not certain how important such variation among song types is to the birds. We do know, however, that birds in the same neighborhood of territories coalesce in their singing around a common song type and can distinguish this repertoire from taped playbacks of songs from titmice singing only a few kilometers away.

Black-crested Titmice have a song repertoire of about ten songs, about half as many as the Tufted Titmouse. Again, the most common song is *peter-peter-peter,* but the second note of each phrase is usually rendered at a *higher* pitch than the first, contrary to the song of the Tufted Titmouse.

Female titmice also sing periodically, although the function of such song is less clear than that of male song. Male and female titmice often pair for life and remain together throughout the nonbreeding season. I once live-trapped the male of a pair, a bird I could sex because I had previously heard him sing and knew that when a pair is together, only the male sings. While I was measuring and banding him, his female began to sing persistently. Could such behavior, then, be used to locate a female's missing mate, or perhaps to advertise her new availability?

Vocalizations other than song are collectively described simply as calls. These are given by both sexes and have been divided by researcher Keith Dixon into ten different varieties employed by the birds in different contexts. The most common is quite chickadee-like, rendered sometimes as *tschk-day* or *tsee-day-day-day,* and is thought to serve as a contact note among birds foraging through a woodland. The dominant male of a flock often gives this call repeatedly as the group assembles first thing in the morning from their dispersed roosting places.

A second major variety of call is used more often in the close proximity of other titmice. One variation, *see-cheyay,* serves as a male's challenge to another male in the same flock. A second variation, *tsee-chup,* apparently is directed mostly toward the mate. A third variation, *see-see-dyih,* has been uttered by birds engaging in a border dispute with their neighbors.

A quite musical note, rendered as *tee-pleur,* is given during actual fighting. In south Texas, I once listened to two border-fighting Black-crested Titmice utter this sound as they fell to the ground in each other's clutches. They eventually disengaged from their wrestling match and flew off to their respective territories only after the two of them were landed on by a third titmouse.

Titmice also have a very soft contact note, *sit* or *tsit,* that is given by birds in close proximity. This call seems to function to keep birds, particularly members of the same pair, aware of each other's location while minimizing the chances of being located by a predator such as a hawk. In the winter, other species, such as the cardinal, also give contact calls. Researcher Kim Sullivan showed that when she played such calls to Downy Woodpeckers, the woodpeckers spent less time looking out for predators. This shows that the woodpeckers rely on the vigilance of other species, as indicated by the presence of their calls, to warn them against predators and use the time they save to forage more steadily for their own food supply.

Two other calls are associated more directly with predators. A very high-pitched *see-see-see* expresses mild alarm or warning and is often given in response to an overflying hawk. A loud, continuous squeal is given whenever a titmouse is held by a researcher or, presumably, by a predator. Researcher Geoffrey Hill used a tape recorder to play such squeal calls to free-ranging groups of titmice. The birds approached the recorder slowly and cautiously. When he paired the recording with a hawk model, the birds did not approach as closely. Hill concluded that the adaptive function of the squealing call was to warn other titmice of the presence of a predator rather than to call for help. As young titmice often remain with their parents over the winter, perhaps such behavior has evolved because the birds being warned are often relatives.

The position of the crest seems to be an important visual communication signal. Lowered crests often are accompanied by sleeked body plumage, the two signals together serving to make the bird as small and, perhaps, unthreatening as possible.

The bird pictured here is in the midst of a visual display termed wing quivering. This conspicuous behavior is rendered in several social contexts and is marked by rapid and shallow movements of the wings, with the tail contracted and lowered. Often, but not always, a soft *tsee-tsee-tsee* call accompanies the motion.

Wing quivering can be seen in both members of a pair during the female's fertile period, the period of the reproductive season when she ovulates one egg per day to be fertilized in her oviduct. At that time of year, this display is often followed by copulation, an event that occurs three or four times per day. The two birds may begin a copulation sequence by facing each other while they both wing-quiver. Then the male maneuvers behind and onto the female and fertilizes her by sperm transfer as their cloacas come into contact.

During and after the female's fertile period, she often wing-quivers at the male's approach in expectation of being fed by him. Such behavior has been termed courtship feeding, a rather inaccurate term, since the male also feeds his female after all the eggs have been laid and she is incubating the clutch. In fact, such feeding seems to be an adaptive method for the male to contribute to the production of the young.

Large food items are gripped in the claws while being torn into smaller pieces with the bill. One investigator has calculated that a male prepares and feeds the female enough food to cover the cost in energy and nutrients of producing the one egg she lays per day. Only the female of the pair incubates, so by feeding her during the incubation period, the male also benefits, because such feeding allows the female to incubate for longer periods rather than having to break off incubation to search for her own food. The eggs thus hatch more quickly.

Finally, the same sort of wing quivering, along with begging vocalizations, is prominently displayed by young titmice recently out of the nest. During their first several days after leaving the nest, known as fledging, the young perch amid the vegetation near the cavity and wing-quiver whenever a parent comes into sight.

3

The Nonbreeding Season

Beyond identifying birds and admiring their beauty is a wonderful world of intellectual inquiry about their lives. To the ecologist, this inquiry centers on two tasks. The first task is to identify patterns in nature—for example, that female songbirds often prefer to mate with males that sing a greater-than-average variety of songs. (This may or may not be true for titmice; we know it is for other songbird species.) The second task is to try to understand why such a pattern exists. Why might females, such as the one pictured here among the blossoms of a red maple, prefer males with more song types?

The search for the answer to questions such as this one immediately plunges us into evolutionary biology, the unifying theme of all biology. Evolutionary theory assumes that animals have evolved to maximize their lifetime reproductive success. For now, we will assume that this means they have been selected for characteristics that maximize the number of offspring they produce during their lifetime. A shorthand way of saying this is that they maximize their fitness. In the case of mate selection that we are considering here, we assume that females mating with males that sing many songs leave more offspring per lifetime—that is, they are more fit.

Why do we need to think this way about titmouse biology? As the rest of this book will demonstrate, thinking in terms of natural selection and evolution serves to make clear many otherwise puzzling attributes of titmice.

The successive generations of animals of any species present an endless spiral of birth, reproduction, and death. In this book, I have chosen to tap the titmouse spiral at the point when a young bird fledges—that is, when it leaves the nest, as this one is about to do. For the next several days, it does little other than sit quietly near the nest and beg strenuously for food using the wing-quiver display every time one of its parents comes into view. After a few days, it begins to take short flights and starts to peck at objects in its environment, most of which it finds are not edible. It also learns about predators by associating the alarm calls of its parents with certain objects in its environment, such as hawks and cats.

The young titmouse gradually wing-quivers less over the next few weeks, becoming nutritionally independent from its parents as its proficiency at finding food increases. This post-fledging period is one of great risk for young birds. Although we do not have satisfactory records for titmice, work with other songbirds indicates that in the days just after leaving the nest, a substantial number of young are taken by both mammal and hawk predators. It is not known whether those young that survive have learned to better identify predators or are just lucky. The second major source of death for birds during their first summer is starvation. In one study with juncos, Kim Sullivan found that starvation was common a number of weeks after fledging and just after the young birds became independent from their parents for their food supply.

We assume that natural selection favors characteristics that increase survivorship. Survivorship is difficult to measure and even more difficult to relate to particular titmouse characteristics or environmental forces. It should be closely related to nutritional condition, however—titmice that are in good nutritional condition will be more likely to survive than titmice in poor nutritional condition. Historically, nutritional condition has been indexed by body mass; the heavier the bird, the better its nutritional condition. But now there is a new method for indexing nutritional condition that has proven useful in research on titmouse biology.

Look carefully at the tail of this titmouse. There is a rather faint progression of alternating dark and light bands perpendicular to the long axis of the tail. The combination of one light band and an adjacent dark band is called a growth bar. Such growth bars are found on almost all feathers of all species of birds. Sometimes such bars are obscured by pigment bars, but the growth bars themselves are found on uniformly colored feathers. They are even found on pure white feathers.

A growth bar denotes twenty-four hours' growth of the feather. So by measuring the width of a growth bar, one can determine the rate at which the feather was grown. If we pull out one tail feather, the bird will regenerate that feather, and we can assume that natural selection will favor regrowing such an important feather as rapidly as possible. (A fully grown feather is held in the follicle solely by dead connective tissue, so pulling the feather presumably causes a bird very little, if any, discomfort.) Now, suppose we recapture the bird some weeks later and pull out the newly regenerated feather. By measuring the growth bars, we can tell how fast that regenerated feather was grown. Since natural selection favors growth as fast as possible, if the feather grows slowly, we can assume the bird was not in very good nutritional condition. In fact, a laboratory study of Carolina Chickadees demonstrated that the rate of feather growth was related to how much food a bird had available to it. I call this new method for indexing nutritional condition ptilochronology, meaning "the study of feather time." Ptilochronology has allowed us to explore how a number of titmouse characteristics might be related to nutritional condition and, by extension, to survivorship.

Dispersal is usually defined as an animal's movement between where it is born and where it breeds. We know quite a bit about the lives of birds throughout the year, except for one or more brief dispersal intervals after they leave their birth site. The dispersal movement that takes place between the place where a bird is born and the place it first breeds is termed natal dispersal. By contrast, breeding dispersal refers to movements between successive breeding sites. Most of the young titmice produced from any one nesting attempt leave their parents' territory several weeks after fledging. One day they are there, the next day they are gone. Researchers place colored plastic bands on the legs of young birds in hopes of studying natal dispersal. Only a very small percentage of such young are ever seen again. Do the rest die? Do they disperse too far to be found? We have very poor information bearing on these questions.

This young bird has paused from its dispersal journey in late September to rest among Virginia creeper vines. We know virtually nothing about the behavior of dispersing young titmice. I once noticed three such juveniles moving through a woodland together. Do brothers and sisters start out together? If so, how long do they stay together? Do they follow certain dispersal paths, such as along fencerows or riverine woodlands?

How wide a gap of unhospitable habitat are dispersing titmice willing cross? That is, what are their gap-crossing tendencies? This is an important matter for the species' range. Consider the Lake Erie islands. Lake Erie is completely surrounded by the range of the Tufted Titmouse, but the major islands of the Lake Erie archipelago have no titmice. Why? These islands are covered with deciduous woodlands, and furthermore, they are occupied by many people who feed birds in the winter. Dispersing titmice must be unwilling to cross the 2 to 3 mile water gap between the mainland and the nearest island, even though there is little doubt about their ability to do so. All the major islands of the Lake Erie archipelago have Black-capped Chickadees, however. This chickadee species may be less reluctant than the titmouse to cross water, or the island populations may be a relict of the late Pleistocene, when the islands were still connected to the mainland.

How do dispersing titmice decide when to stop? We know that they spend the winter in a flock with a pair of adult titmice that are not their relatives. We also know from intense banding studies of other species of chickadees and titmice that young males disperse shorter distances from the birth site than young females. Why is this? In the Marsh Tit, a European relative of our titmouse, Swedish researcher Jan-Åke Nilsson has demonstrated that the earlier of two dispersers to join a winter social group will be socially dominant. We also know that birds socially dominant within a winter flock will have a greater chance of breeding in the area the following spring.

One idea to explain the adaptiveness of the shorter dispersal distance in males is that social dominance status in the winter flock is more important for males than for females, so males should spend less time than females in choosing a flock to join. When females form a pair-bond with a male, they assume the same dominance rank as their new mate. Because their dominance status is not determined so importantly by when they join a group, they can afford to be more choosy about finding a flock living in high-quality habitat. Thus, we find the females settling farther from their birth site than males.

It may also be that some genetically determined behavior is related to how far a titmouse disperses. We know from studies with long-distance migrant birds that the number of days when they show a particular kind of restlessness related to migration is genetically determined. Perhaps the amount of dispersal-like behavior in titmice differs between males and females. As far as I know, this matter of dispersal-related restlessness has not been studied in any nonmigratory bird species.

In most species, the young birds leave their parents' territory at the beginning of the dispersal period in late summer. Tufted Titmice are almost unique among all titmice and chickadees in that not all young disperse. In fact, we now are reasonably sure that very often one young bird actually stays with its parents through the winter following its birth and may actually help them rear its younger brothers and sisters.

A few good records based on banded birds have shown yearling titmice bringing food to their young siblings. Such helping behavior by birds that are not actually breeding has been termed cooperative breeding. Among titmice, only the Tufted Titmouse and the Black Tit of Africa are known to be cooperative breeders, but it may not be too long before someone finds this trait in the Black-crested Titmouse, and I expect it will be discovered in many of the African tits. Among birds as a whole, cooperative breeding is not uncommon. It is found worldwide in many taxonomic familes and seems concentrated in species living at low latitudes.

Before such cooperative breeding can occur, the dominant territorial pair must allow the helper to remain in their territory. The case in which a pair allows one of their youngsters from one year to stay with them over the following nonbreeding season has been termed offspring retention by Swedish ecologist Jan Ekman. Ekman makes a strong case that before cooperative breeding could have evolved, offspring retention must have been favored by natural selection. Under what conditions would such retention have been selected for? The argument assumes that, as with many behavioral patterns, adult birds should allow an offspring to remain only if the benefits of doing so exceed the costs. Ekman believes that the principal benefit to the adults is that they can help their retained young survive better than if it were out on its own, thus increasing their own reproductive success. However, the cost is that that same youngster will be consuming food in their territory all through the winter months.

According to Ekman's hypothesis, in late summer and early autumn, the parents somehow assess the amount of food in their territory. If there is sufficient food to feed an additional mouth in the territory, they should retain the offspring. However, if the previous growing season has been a poor one or if they have a very small territory, they should force the young bird to disperse by continually being aggressive toward it and chasing it about until it leaves their territory. Why is only one young bird retained, when it is not uncommon for six or eight young to leave the nest? After a time, the young birds become intolerant of one another, and the most dominant youngster, usually the largest male, may actually force all his brothers and sisters to disperse.

This fledgling Black-crested Titmouse is eating a spider it has found in its parents' territory. How might we evaluate Ekman's idea about the adaptive reasons for titmice retaining their offspring? The crucial issue is the balance between food supply and number of consumers during the nonbreeding season. Suppose food, such as a sunflower seed feeder, is added to a titmouse territory early in the breeding season. The territorial pair might take into account this superabundant food supply when determining the total amount of food in their territory. Therefore, because the parents would conclude that they had a rich food reserve, we might expect offspring retention to be more common in territories with sunflower seed feeders than in territories without them.

Conversely, suppose we live-trap in the autumn any young titmouse that has been retained by its parents. We might cause such a young bird to "disperse" by letting it go in a woodland some miles away from its parents' territory, far enough away that it will not return. Because we have removed the young bird, there should be considerably less demand on the food supply in its parents' territory, so the parents should remain in better nutritional condition through the winter than the adults in other territories where we have not removed the young birds.

By measuring the width of growth bars on induced feathers, we can access nutritional condition in free-ranging birds, so it is possible to investigate the effect of removing the young bird on the parents' nutrition by indexing the rate at which parents with and without young in their territory regenerate one tail feather. As I write this, Elena Pravosudova and I are performing the above experiments with Tufted Titmice, but as yet we have no definitive answer to report.

When a young titmouse disperses in the autumn from its natal territory, assuming it does not die of starvation and is not taken by a predator, where does it stop for the winter, and why? We assume that natural selection favors behavior that brings the young titmouse to the start of the next breeding season with both a breeding site and a mate. The first priority is survival. The Tufted Titmouse is a mast specialist—a species that concentrates in areas with abundant mast crops, acorns and beechnuts in the case of titmice, and relies on such mast for much of its winter food supply. This bird is sitting in a pine tree and may eventually settle for the winter at a site with some coniferous trees, but under natural conditions, wintering titmice are not found far from mast crops.

Titmice use their bills to pound open beechnuts, pin oak acorns, and shingle oak acorns while holding them between their feet. We do not know the maximum acorn size they can handle. Larger acorns, such as those from red oaks, might be too big for them to carry in their bills and quite possibly too hard for them to peck open. Titmice are not totally precluded from using the large acorns, however. They often rummage around on the ground in the leavings of squirrels, gleaning bits of nut meat from the broken shells.

Ornithologists have long treated the length of the bill as an invariant attribute of an individual bird—that is, an individual bird's bill length would measure the same at any time of the year. The Great Titmouse of Eurasia, shown below, is the ecological equivalent of our titmice in winter. It forages on the ground for mast, which it pounds open in the same way as our titmice.

English ornithologist Andy Gosler has recently found that male Great Titmice in England have shorter bills in the winter than in the summer. He attributes the difference to increased bill wear in the winter as the birds pound open seed after seed. Interestingly, the difference in bill length is much less in females, which eat fewer large, heavy seeds than males. The males use their socially dominant status to deny adult females, as well as young birds of both sexes, access to large seeds.

It sometimes happens that local patches of beech or pin oak trees can have a superabundant mast crop. In such cases, large numbers of dispersing young titmice can congregate for the winter into roving, nonterritorial juvenile gangs. Sometimes these groups are quite spectacular. While the normal flock size of wintering titmice is three to five, gangs can consist of as many as twenty-five to thirty.

A young bird must escape predators if it is to survive to breed. Knowing that they have evolved as mast specialists and that beech, pin oak, and shingle oak all have the trait of keeping their brownish leaves through most of the winter, we can see the adaptiveness of titmouse coloration. The gray and russet plumage effectively camouflages the bird against the tree bark and foliage. A titmouse flying from the ground into such a tree seems to disappear instantly from view. It is also hidden from the view of Sharp-shinned and Cooper's Hawks, the principal daytime predators of titmice. It is interesting to note that many of the Asian and African tits that live among evergreen vegetation are much more greenish to greenish gray in plumage color.

Besides food and protection from daytime predators, habitat selected by young dispersers must have adequate nocturnal roosting sites. This is an interesting and underexplored matter. It seems quite possible that another "cost-benefit analysis" is involved. During warmer weather, titmice roost at night within bark curls and on branches next to trunks, where they are rather exposed to the environment but can fly off in most any direction if approached by a nighttime predator such as a weasel.

In very cold weather, titmice roost inside holes in trees and other cavity sites. Do the titmice choose such sites to gain protection from the cold weather, even though any escape route would be blocked by an oncoming predator? Simple experiments with artificial roost sites of various configurations could help answer this question.

After locating a suitable place to spend the winter, a young titmouse must join the existing titmouse social system. Titmouse flocks are marked by what is called a peck-right dominance hierarchy, a term coined by ecologist W. C. Allee, who first noticed such hierarchies in flocks of chickens. In a peck-right hierarchy, the dominance-subordinance relation between any two individual birds is constant and fixed. That is, one of the two birds always has the "right" to peck or dominate the other. Allee described another form of hierarchy, called a peck-dominance hierarchy, in which dominance is only relative. Here one bird dominates the other in a majority of encounters, but not all of them.

It is easy to tell which of two titmice at a feeder has the "peck right" over the other. Most obviously, a bird is dominant to a second if it chases it or takes its place at a perch site. This second form of dominance is termed a supplanting attack. More subtly, one bird may wait at a perch until a dominant has finished getting a seed or using a suet feeder. Here, a subordinate titmouse is fluttering at the side of the feeder while the dominant boldly comes for a seed. When individual birds are given uniquely identifying marks, such as colored plastic leg bands, it can be seen that there is almost always a single dominance hierarchy within a flock. The alpha, or most dominant, bird is the male that bred in the area the past

season. In essence, he is still on his territory but has allowed titmice besides his mate to stay over the winter. The most subordinate bird is a newly arrived young female. The rest of the birds are of intermediate dominance status. In general, in one-on-one encounters, all males dominate all females, and the female who bred in the area the previous summer dominates all younger females.

We have no information on how dominance relations are formed among young Tufted or Black-crested Titmice. However, Jan-Åke Nilsson and his colleagues in Sweden have studied the matter in a relative of our titmouse, the Marsh Tit.

In that species, shown at right center, the first young bird to arrive at a site is usually dominant over all later arrivals of the same sex. When two birds of the same sex arrive at a site at more or less the same time, the larger of the two dominates the smaller. There are two lessons here. First, it should be adaptive for titmice to breed as early in the year as they can so that their offspring disperse early. Early dispersers find available winter flocks first and therefore become socially dominant. Second, it is adaptive to produce big offspring, since that confers additional dominance potential. One way to produce big offspring is to fertilize or become fertilized by a big partner, whether a social mate or not. This second matter has some fascinating implications that will be explored further in chapter 4.

Why might it be adaptive to be socially dominant? First, the dominant birds exert their status regarding the food supply. It is not uncommon to see a dominant bird supplant a subordinate from a site where the latter seems to be finding food. Many times I have watched a dominant take a beechnut or acorn from a subordinate. Also, the dominant pair of birds has breeding rights to the area the following spring. All subordinates must again disperse in search of their own breeding locale.

Within a titmouse flock, the males and females are arranged into dominance-ordered pairs, but the pairs seem to be temporary. What happens if the dominant female is taken by a weasel? The second female, called the beta female, divorces the beta male and pairs with the newly widowed alpha male. The gamma female moves up to pair with the newly divorced beta male. It may be that this system of moving up the ladder can explain the flock size of wintering titmice.

Since only the dominant pair breeds at the site, a young bird can breed there only if all more-dominant members of its sex die during the winter. So the probability of breeding is equal to the chance of each more-dominant bird dying times the number of more-dominant birds. Clearly, it would not pay to join a very large flock. The only exception seems to be the roving gangs at super-abundant mast crops. It would be interesting to know if such gangs were composed of inferior birds that would never achieve high dominance rank in a normal winter flock.

Anyone with a bird feeder knows that titmice are not alone in using it. They are joined by a dozen or so familiar backyard bird species. Such species have been divided by ecologists into foraging guilds, groups of species that search for food in similar places and in a similar fashion. Such species as Northern Cardinals, Tree Sparrows, Dark-eyed Juncos, Song Sparrows, House Sparrows, and House Finches are assigned to the ground-foraging guild. Titmice, chickadees, nuthatches, Brown Creepers, and woodpeckers, which do most of their foraging on trees and shrubs, have been designated the bark-foraging guild, sometimes called the arboreal-foraging guild or tree-foraging guild.

During their autumn migration period, a number of warblers and other species associate temporarily with Tufted Titmice during migration stopovers. Yellow-rumped Warblers and Golden-crowned Kinglets can be found foraging with titmice and chickadees even into December in my area of Ohio. In Texas, many of these same species associate throughout the winter with Black-crested Titmice. In the Santa Ana National Wildlife Refuge along the Rio Grande, I have watched Black-crested Titmice leading flocks containing kinglets, gnatcatchers, and pewees, as well as warblers and vireos.

From observations solely at feeding stations, it would not be possible to tell whether titmice and the other bark-foraging species, such as this Northern Cardinal, truly form foraging groups by mutual attraction or whether they are together at the feeders simply because they are attracted independently to the food supply. However, anyone walking through the winter woods will find that these species really are attracted to each other. They follow one another and maintain a cohesive flock in a relatively small space, while all around them the remainder of the woodland is empty of birds.

Just as within a species, a social dominance hierarchy exists among the species in the bark-foraging guild. The cross-species hierarchy is sometimes peck-right and sometimes peck-dominance, both hierarchies based mainly on relative size. For example, Hairy Woodpeckers always dominate Downy Wood-peckers, downies dominate White-breasted Nuthatches, and nuthatches the resident chickadee species. Titmice always dominate chickadees, but the relationship between White-breasted Nuthatches and titmice is more complicated. Usually the nuthatch is socially dominant to the titmouse, but sometimes a grizzled old male titmouse is socially dominant to a young female nuthatch, so overall the issue between the two species is peck-dominance.

Why has natural selection favored such mixed-species flocking? What is adaptive about such mutual attraction? These questions have provoked a good deal of discussion. There are two theories, both of which assume that natural selection favors behavior that increases the ratio of fitness benefits to costs.

As it bends down to peck at a food item, this titmouse is unaware of an approaching hawk. The first theory on the advantage of foraging in mixed-species groups is that by foraging with other birds, an individual reduces its chances of being taken by a predator. A hawk has many potential targets instead of just one, and if the hawk is spotted and the flock all dives for cover at once, the hawk may be confused by so many potential targets. Also, if all the birds in a group are periodically scanning the environment for predators, a behavior termed vigilance, the chances are good that at least one bird would see any approaching predator before it was too close.

The titmouse here is being vigilant by looking out for predators prior to removing a seed. The other theory about the advantages of mixed-species foraging relates to an increased ability to find food. A bird of one species may see a bird of another find food in a novel location and copy its behavior. Also, because all the birds in the group are periodically scanning for predators, each individual need not spend as much of its own time being vigilant. The time saved from vigilance can then be spent on finding additional food.

Why might it be adaptive for a titmouse to forage with other species rather than just with members of its own species? Birds of the same species are each other's closest competitors for food. They look for food in the same places and use the same foraging methods. By foraging with members of other species, a bird can reap the benefits of social foraging and not suffer the cost of competing for food with many members of its own species. Along with the low chance of subordinates getting breeding territories in the spring, this food competition among members of the same species should operate to keep titmouse flocks small.

A titmouse maintains a frozen posture for several minutes after a hawk-alarm call is given by a member of a mixed-species flock. It may be that some of the consequences of mixed-species flocking could increase the chances of titmice surviving, while other consequences could decrease the chances. We would expect mixed-species flocking to be maintained by natural selection only if the benefits outweighed the costs. For example, suppose titmice could reduce their predation risk if they foraged with nuthatches but suffered nutritionally because the socially dominant nuthatches kept displacing them from newly found food items.

No tests of relative costs and benefits of mixed-species flocking have been done with titmice, but David Cimprich and I have performed such a test with chickadees. Titmice, which are socially dominant to chickadees, use such dominance to displace chickadees from food items and to force the chickadees to forage in less-preferred parts of a tree. Cimprich and I theorized that if there were a nutritional cost to chickadees of foraging with titmice, then if we removed the titmice, the remaining chickadees would regenerate a tail feather faster, showing wider growth bars, than if the titmice were not removed. That is exactly what happened. In woodlots where we removed all the titmice, the regenerated chickadee feathers had wider growth bars. So we showed that the chickadees paid a nutritional cost for being in the company of titmice. The benefit-cost ratio for the chickadees might still have been positive, though, if the chickadees received considerable warning from predators in the larger flock. Also, it is possible that the nutritional cost to the chickadees would have been even higher if they had continually tried to evade the titmice rather than flocked with them.

Once the young titmouse has selected an area in which to spend the winter and has determined its dominance position, how does it look for food and what does it eat? A mast specialist, it spends a considerable portion of its time searching the leaf litter for acorns or beechnuts. Here in central Ohio, my student Vladimir Pravosudov recorded titmice foraging on the ground in 27 percent of sightings. The species appears adapted to cope with snow cover by caching a great many food items in the trees earlier in the autumn.

Titmice are omnivores, with a diet containing both plant and animal items. In their large monograph on the food habits of wildlife, Alexander Martin and his coworkers reported that over the five cold-weather months, the diet of the titmice they examined was 78 percent vegetable material and 22 percent animal. The analogous percentages for plant material in spring, summer, and fall, respectively, were 11, 18, and 39 percent. Of the vegetable items, oak and beech mast was most important, but also recorded were pine seeds and the fruits of blueberry, blackberry, mulberry, bayberry, Virginia creeper, and hackberry.

Much of the animal material in the timouse diet consists of insects found by closely examining the surface of shrubs and trees. In the Martin study, caterpillars made up over half the annual consumption of animal food, with wasps also making up a large portion of the diet. Scale insects, spiders, beetles, and ants constituted minor components. The acrobatic birds sometimes search for insects on the underside of limbs in much the same way that this bird (top photo) is getting seeds from the underside of a feeder.

Some years ago, I recorded the proportion of time that titmice wintering in a woodland in northern New Jersey spent looking for food on different parts of trees. I found that in calm, rather mild weather, almost 90 percent of their time was spent searching for food items on branches less than 5 centimeters in diameter. Why was this? Do the titmice really seek out such branch sizes, or were they just foraging at random in woodlands where 90 percent of the possible places to forage were less than 5 centimeters in diameter?

In order to investigate this question, Virginia Pierce and I dismantled a large American elm tree, cutting it up into 1-meter-long branches of different diameter, and hung sixty such branches in a large indoor aviary. We then introduced single titmice to the aviary and recorded which branch sizes they preferred to search for food. The answer was quite clear: They preferred to forage on branches in the 2.5 and 5-centimeter categories much more than would be expected based on either total length or total surface area of the six branch-diameter classes we used.

Wintering titmice use behavior to save energy while foraging. In hilly terrain, they are much more common on south slopes during sunny weather, presumably to take advantage of the warmth provided by solar radiation. Bill Shields and I found that 95 percent of all titmice we sighted in a northern New Jersey forest during one winter were located on south slopes.

Out here in the great flatlands of the Midwest, there is little chance to capitalize on topography. In fact, many of our titmice are confined to isolated woodlots in a flat sea of cornfields. During the winter, such habitats become quite stressful thermally because of the combination of low temperature and high winds. Nevertheless, the birds have several methods of reducing such stress by reducing their exposure to wind. First, they spend more time near and on the ground in very cold weather. In the coldest, windiest weather I recorded in one project, titmice spent fully 80 percent of their foraging time within 2 meters of the ground.

Though there are no hills to use as windbreaks, there are small stream valleys in the woodlots I studied. In the coldest weather, the titmice spent 100 percent of their time in these little shelters, foraging for insects and seeds under the overhanging stream banks. As might be expected, in colder, windier weather, the birds stayed away from the windward edge of the woodlots more than in more benign weather. The titmice even capitalized on small windbreaks throughout the woods. When it became colder or windier, they confined themselves to looking for food only close to the leeward side of individual large trees. Finally, the birds seemed to reduce cold stress by flying less. We can think of a flying bird as creating its own wind speed. The titmice moved less rapidly through the woods as the temperature dropped. Between 52 and 68 degrees Fahrenheit (10 and 20 degrees Celsius), they moved 30 meters per minute, but in temperatures between 4 and –14 degrees F (–10 and –20 degrees C), they moved only about 11 meters per minute.

Wintering titmice are omnivores. In his monumental series on bird biology, Arthur Cleveland Bent reported that over the course of the year, 66 percent of the diet of titmice was animal and 34 percent vegetable. We do not know whether this is by choice. For example, if you put out both mealworms and sunflower seeds in your feeder, would an individual titmouse take a balanced diet or go solely for one or the other food type? There have been attempts to determine which of several seed types titmice prefer. The bird shown here is leaving a feeder after having selected a safflower seed. Titmice and chickadees are quite adept at clamping food items against a branch with their feet and then using their rather stout bills to pound and tear the items into bitesize morsels. In one English study, titmice readily learned to pull up a string with their bill and feet in combination to reach a seed glued to the end.

Fats, or lipids, contain about twice as much energy per gram or ounce as proteins or carbohydrates. Titmice and other warm-blooded animals require more energy to maintain their body temperature in colder weather than they do in warmer weather. Particularly on cold days, titmice will take a meal of suet, which is essentially pure fat. I believe that you could construct a kind of titmouse suet "virtual" thermometer by taking careful notes on how often backyard titmice use a suet feeder per hour and comparing those amounts with the current temperatures.

This titmouse is having a meal of fox grapes during early autumn. By early winter, however, most wild berry crops are gone, eaten by migrating hordes of robins, thrushes, and waxwings. Although I have watched chickadees and Downy Woodpeckers eating the berries of poison ivy throughout the winter, I have never seen titmice use this food source.

Titmice do not immediately consume all the food they find. Particularly in the autumn and winter, they hide, or cache, many such items in their territory. Titmice are called scatter hoarders, which means that they cache food items throughout their territory, stuffing them behind curls of bark, wedging them behind cracks in a tree trunk, or even burying them in the ground. By contrast, some other birds, most notably the Red-headed Woodpecker, are called larder hoarders. They concentrate all their caches within one or two trees in the autumn, and then defend their caches against all other animals over the course of the winter. Scatter hoarders do not attempt to defend every cached item. Instead, they apparently spread the caches far enough apart that other animals have difficulty finding them at more than a chance rate.

Some birds, particularly members of the jay and titmouse families, can remember for weeks or even months the precise locations where they have cached individual food items. Some researchers think that this memory ability is associated with enlargement of a particular area of the brain, the hippocampus, known to be associated with spatial learning. Very often, just after caching a food item, a titmouse will seem to stare at the item and then at the immediate surroundings. Could the bird be memorizing the location?

Birds stop caching from the same food source after they have deposited a large number of caches in the immediate vicinity. Why is this? Why do they not just pack the surrounding trees full of food items? One idea is that by keeping the caches spread out, they reduce the chances of another animal finding one cache by chance and then searching the immediate vicinity to find many more caches. You can test this theory in your backyard. Move your feeder as far away from its present location as you can, so that the birds will have new places to cache, and then watch to see if the caching rate goes up. You could measure caching rate as either the number of seeds cached per hour or the percentage of all seeds taken from the feeder that are cached.

The primary force of natural selection during most of the winter is to promote characteristics that allow titmice to survive from one day to the next. Unraveling all the adaptations involved is a fascinating business. The birds have two primary forces to deal with: starvation risk and predation risk. Death by starvation probably occurs mostly at night. Each day, titmice build up their fat reserves during the day and metabolize the fat throughout the night to stay warm while they cannot feed. This titmouse, just flying to its roost site at dusk, weighs about 2 grams more than it will when it wakes up the next morning. The 2-gram difference is the fat supply that will be used up during the night.

Titmice have several methods to conserve their energy supply. During very cold weather, you may have seen titmice sitting on their feet with their feathers erected. Both of these behavioral patterns increase the bird's insulation layer to reduce heat loss to the environment. A second way some members of the titmouse family save energy is by reducing their body temperature while roosting at night by going into nocturnal hypothermia.

During nocturnal hypothermia, a bird allows its body temperature to fall as much as 10 or 12 degrees F (5 or 6 degrees C) below the normal daytime level. Such hypothermia can save as much as 10 percent of the energy expended through the night. Nocturnal hypothermia has not been shown to exist in Tufted or Black-crested Titmice, but I would be very surprised if it were absent in those species.

It appears that predation risk, the other major determinant of winter survival, has two very different components. In the daytime, predation is by hawks, and risk is likely reduced by foraging in flocks. We know much less about nighttime predation, but nocturnal mammals such as weasels are probably the chief predators.

Titmice have two major sources of energy during the winter: their internal body fat and their external caches. They build up and draw down both of these energy sources, thus engaging in energy management. We are just now beginning to understand the complexity of such management. We do not know whether the titmice have any kind of conscious management policy, but the following is an example of the theoretical issues involved.

Suppose a titmouse is living in a habitat with a large population of hawks, so its daytime predation risk is high. The theory says the titmouse should react by carrying less weight, partially so it will be more maneuverable and harder for a hawk to catch. In such a risky habitat, then, perhaps a titmouse keeps more of its energy reserves as caches and less as body fat. If it keeps its weight lower, it must go to roost with less fat, so its risk of starving during the night is higher. But then it could go deeper into hypothermia to reduce fat consumption at night to make up the deficit. A bird deep in hypothermia may be less likely to detect an oncoming weasel, however, so its risk of nocturnal predation goes up. What about a reserve for the morning? Suppose it wakes up to find its foraging sites covered with ice, as shown above. Does the titmouse allow for this possibility by always retaining some body fat for the next day? It has recently been shown in the European Nuthatch that the birds use their caches only during cold, windy weather, so during ice storms titmice may rely heavily on cached items.

A number of research groups around the world are studying how wintering birds such as titmice manage their energy supplies. The titmouse here is feeding on cornmeal paste spread onto the trunk of a cherry tree. One study in our laboratory is attempting to discover whether body fat and caches are managed in a compensatory manner. For example, what happens if we allow a titmouse to feed only on food items too small to cache, such as this cornmeal? Wiill it compensate for the lack of caches by increasing its body fat? The answer so far has been somewhat surprising: the titmice do not compensate, suggesting that fat supply does not depend on cache supply. But perhaps fat supply does influence the tendency to cache. Jeffrey Lucas, a leading researcher in this field, has evidence that titmice and chickadees seem to cache only when their fat supply is at adequate levels.

Through adaptations for reducing predation risk and starvation risk, titmice increase their chances of surviving the winter. With the onset of spring, a second set of adaptive responses comes into play, those concerned with producing the maximum possible number of young that will, in turn, survive and reproduce. Let's now consider the biology of titmice during the breeding season.

4

The Breeding Season

With migrant bird species, we can easily define the start of the breeding season as the day the first bird arrives on the breeding ground. No such clear-cut starting point is detectable in most permanent-resident birds. Instead, with the waning of winter, there is a gradual increase in aggression and intolerance within winter flocks. The aggression is a product of increasing concentrations of testosterone, which is in response to increasing day length.

Eventually, the increase in aggressiveness has the effect of dividing the wintering flocks into pairs or pairs plus helpers, each occupying a breeding territory. Margaret Morse Nice, a pioneer student of bird ecology, suggests that there are several different types of bird breeding territory, depending on their function. According to her scheme, Tufted and Black-crested Titmice occupy a Type I territory, one that furnishes all the requisites for breeding. In a Type I territory, the nest and food supply are located entirely within the territorial boundaries. In contrast, the Red-winged Blackbird has a Type II territory, in which the birds locate the nest within the territory but go off the territory to obtain their food supplies.

Here in Ohio, the switch between quiet flocking and aggressive intolerance leading to territory formation can be seen on a daily basis as early as mid-February. Particularly on bright, sunny days, once the alpha male has obtained the requisite amount of food, he begins to sing loudly and chase the subordinate males about the flock home range.

The intolerance of the dominant male and female probably is a powerful inducement for surbordinate birds to leave their winter home range and begin searching for breeding sites. This renewed movement, after the winter's hiatus, is called spring dispersal. What causes birds to begin dispersing and to move as far as they do before settling down again is not well understood. Titmice often disperse as male-female pairs that were formed over the course of the winter, but dispersal by individual birds is not uncommon. Much of the loud singing heard late in the spring appears to be unmated males advertising to attract single dispersing females. Some young titmice do not disperse in the spring. Such juveniles remain with their parents and later help feed their younger brothers and sisters.

It appears that subordinate pairs will disperse from the winter flock any time they detect a nearby vacancy. When David Cimprich and I removed titmice in our study of chickadee nutritional condition, we sometimes found new pairs of titmice moving into the woodlots in the middle of winter, rather than just during the spring dispersal period. Researcher William Pielou also recorded arrivals of new birds into his Michigan study site during the winter.

During the winter, titmice can be found in the suburbs, frequenting any smallish backyard with a bird feeder. For breeding, however, they seem to prefer larger patches of woodland than those required by chickadees and thus are not as likely to be found breeding in backyards. This may be because the titmouse has more restricted nest-site requirements. Like chickadees, titmice nest only in cavities; however, titmice seem to prefer cavity sites high in large trees, 12 meters high in one Michigan study, whereas chickadees will readily take to cavities even less than 1 meter from the ground. It is possible that there are fewer cavities high in large trees in backyards than in larger woodlands.

Titmice do not excavate their own cavities and seldom use the same cavity for more than one year, so during the early spring a pair spends much of its time searching for and inspecting potential nest cavities. Although this cavity entrance seems to be about the right diameter, the titmouse is likely to reject the site because the limb diameter is too small.

Because titmice withdraw from backyards to breed, usually nest rather high in trees, and seldom use nestboxes, their breeding biology has not been as intensively studied as that of their nestbox-breeding relatives in Europe. Much of our best information on pairs breeding in natural cavities comes from William Pielou's doctoral research in southern Michigan. Pielou found that titmice began inspecting cavities in late April. The female did most of the cavity inspecting while the male perched on a nearby branch. Apparently the kind of tree was not an important consideration, as Pielou recorded titmouse nesting cavities in twenty-one different tree species.

The cavities used by titmice for breeding were old woodpecker holes or places where branch stubs had rotted back into the trunk. They measured 22 to 28 centimeters deep and had entrance holes 4.5 to 5.5 centimeters in diameter. Carolina Chickadee pairs often select more than one cavity and immediately move to a backup cavity if the first breeding attempt is unsuccessful. Titmice may do likewise, but this is as yet unknown. In Pielou's study, no titmice used the same cavity for more than one year. In an earlier review of the study, however, Arthur Cleveland Bent mentioned that titmice would use the same cavity for years if not disturbed.

Soon after the nest site has been selected, the female begins bringing beakfuls of nest material and placing it within the cavity. Pielou noted that the male brought a small percentage of the nest material but never was seen actually building the nest. The male often fed the female during this period. In one pair, the female carried eight loads of material to the nest over the course of forty minutes. On another day, the same female made twenty trips during a two-hour period. The average time for each of seven nests to be built was four days.

There is an orderly progression of nesting materials. Coarser materials such as leaves, moss, strips of bark, and grass are laid down first as a foundation. The nest cup is then formed of softer, more insulative material, such as down, wool, and fur. Titmice may actually pull hairs from dogs and other live mammals and carry them to the nest.

About the time the female is adding the last bits of lining to the nest, her behavior undergoes a remarkable transformation. She begins wing-quivering, along with a persistent and distinctive call termed the begging call. In response, the male begins to bring food items to the female. Such begging and feeding begins at low intensity even while the pair is still looking for cavity sites, but a rapid increase in the intensity of such begging marks the onset of the female's fertile period. During her fertile period, she ovulates one egg per day, and fertilization of that egg occurs in the oviduct. Several times a day, both birds may wing-quiver and vocalize simultaneously, often giving a soft *see* call. Such mutual signaling is usually followed shortly by copulation, which often occurs near the nest site and lasts for only a second or two.

Copulation in titmice occurs several times a day. Pielou observed three copulations by one pair of titmice, occurring at 9:30 A.M., 10:20 A.M., and 2:10 P.M. Pielou records that after two of these copulations, the male engaged in bizarre behavior for which he had no explanation: " . . . . Male remained perched on limb where copulation had occurred. His body was pressed close to the limb so that his legs were concealed. Head and tail were extended in line with the body, eyes gradually closed. He remained in this horizontal position on the branch for a few seconds and then began to tip slowly backward on the limb. His body continued to rotate slowly backward and downward until it was suspended beneath the limb. With eyes still closed in this stuporous state the male then fell toward the ground. After falling about eight feet he suddenly revived and flew off into some nearby bushes. He remained there resting and preening for a few seconds before flying into the woods out of sight."

A female titmouse lays a clutch of three to nine eggs at a rate of one a day. During her fertile period, the female spends the night in the nest cavity. Rather than incubate the eggs in the nest, she perches on the rim of the nest cup and lays one additional egg between 5 and 6 A.M., before leaving the cavity for the first time that day. While the clutch is being formed, she covers the eggs with fur, grass, or both before leaving the cavity.

With the advent of paternity analysis using molecular genetics, mating-system theory has been revolutionized. Formerly, species such as the Tufted and Black-crested Titmice were considered examples of a monogamous mating system, in which one male and one female formed a pair-bond for the purposes of reproduction, and the male that fed the female during her fertile period and then fed the nestlings later on was assumed to be the father of the nestlings. Now we know otherwise. In a great many such species, males often are raising young that they have not fathered, called extra pair young. So now we must distinguish between social and genetic monogamy; the two often are not the same.

Except for the waterfowl, in birds there is no intromittent organ analogous to the mammalian penis. This means that a female bird cannot be copulated with and fertilized against her will. Many researchers believe that the extra pair young in a nest mean that the female of a socially monogamous pair has been favored by natural selection to copulate with and be fertilized by males other than her social mate. Such behavior is thought to confer insurance against infertility in the social mate and to allow the female to mate with males of superior quality even if she has not formed a pair-bond with such mates. The male also should benefit from extra pair copulations if they allow him to produce more offspring.

So the notion of a harmonious pair cooperating to raise their common offspring together no longer exists. It is now thought that females may attempt to be fertilized by males other than their social mates and that males have developed behavior both to fertilize other females and to guard their own females against such extra pair fertilizations. Nothing is yet known about extra pair mating activity in titmice, as the molecular studies are just getting started, although extra pair young have been found in close relatives, such as Black-capped Chickadees in North America and Blue Titmice in Europe.

Much needs to be learned. Can a male tell when he has been cuckolded? If he has been cuckolded, does he work less hard bringing food to the nestlings? How does a female decide to copulate with which other males? One study with the Blue Titmouse in Belgium showed that females flew into neighboring territories to copulate with the resident males, but only if those males were larger than the females' own social mates.

Males apparently have evolved what is called dawn song as an adaptation against becoming cuckolded. During a female's fertile period, her social mate arrives at first light outside the nest cavity where she has been roosting for the night. He sings continually while perched facing the cavity entrance about 10 meters away. Some recent work in Finland with a related species, the Willow Tit, has shown that the male does not stop his dawn song until the female leaves the cavity. This behavior may be a way to let the female know that he is right there and she will not be able to sneak unobserved over to the neighboring male's territory for an extra pair copulation.

The uncertainties about paternity cloud the ability of ecologists to measure lifetime reproductive success. Consider this newly completed clutch of seven eggs in a nestbox. Formerly, if all seven nestlings hatched from these eggs and eventually left the nestbox as fledglings, we would have calculated the reproductive success of the male of the pair as seven. But now we know that his reproductive success may be less than seven if some of these eggs were fathered by another male. Or maybe this male fathered all seven of these eggs and is also the father of eggs in nests belonging to other socially monogamous pairs.

In the future, ecologists will need information on rates of extra pair fertilizations in order to make accurate estimations of lifetime reproductive success in titmice and in all other socially monogamous bird species.

Incidentally, if a strange female laid an egg in this nest, the female would also be raising an offspring that was not her own. However, such "egg dumping" is rare in birds and very rare or absent in most cavity nesters. Thus, the problem of accurately calculating lifetime reproductive success would seem to apply only for male titmice.

The eggs of titmice are ovate to elongate-ovate in shape, with average dimensions of 18.4 millimeters in length and 14.1 millimeters in width. The eggs are white to creamy white and covered with small spots of chestnut, hazel, or light hazel. All the eggs in a clutch are spotted with about the same coloration, but such coloration varies among clutches.

What determines the time of year when a clutch is started and how many eggs it will contain? All else being equal, it would be adaptive for a female to lay early if such behavior resulted in her young becoming independent and dispersing early. If Tufted and Black-crested Titmice are similar to some better-studied tit species, early-dispersing young get better dominance positions in winter flocks and have a higher probability of breeding the following spring. How early a female begins a clutch is limited by her nutrient reserves. It has been shown in European titmice that giving the female extra food in late winter and on into spring will cause her to start laying earlier than normal.

The issue of what determines clutch size is more complicated. Theory says that a bird should lay the number of eggs each year that will maximize her lifetime reproductive success. Up to a point, the more eggs she lays in any one year, the more young she can produce that year. But what if the effort she puts into reproduction reduces her chances of living to the next breeding season? Since natural selection works on lifetime repro-ductive success, not annual reproductive success, the best strategy would consider both annual reproduction and annual survival in determining how large the clutch should be. We would expect larger clutches in richer environments, where the cost to the female in annual survivorship would likely be lower.

During the egg-laying stage, the pair remains away from the nest area throughout the day. Such behavior might be expected if staying nearer the nest increased the probability of its being found by a nest predator such as a squirrel. In order to be sure about this, however, we would need detailed maps of where in their territory the pair spent the day before and during the egg-laying period. This is definitely a doable project.

Curiously, the female begins incubating just after laying the next-to-last egg of the clutch. She stops intensive incubating when the eggs begin to hatch. Since the last egg is incubated one day less than the rest, it often does not hatch, instead becoming buried in the nest material over the succeeding days. In other cases, the last egg does hatch, but later than the rest. Such eggs often give rise to runt nestlings that remain smaller than their siblings. Their late start as nestlings places them at a disadvantage in competition with their brothers and sisters for the food delivered by their parents. In times of food shortage, the runts are the first to starve.

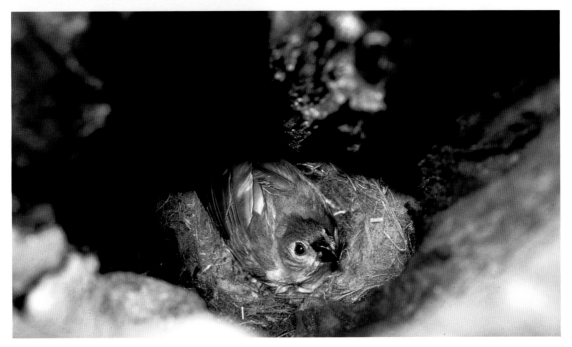

Incubation is carried out entirely by the female and usually lasts for about thirteen days. By the time incubation commences, the feathers over the female's belly have been shed, and the skin of that region has become heavily vascularized with capillary beds. Such a bare, engorged area is called the brood patch and appears to be an adaptation for the efficient transfer of heat from the female's body to the eggs. Males do not have brood patches, which supports the conclusion that the males never incubate. As the female is maintaining not only her own body temperature but also that of the clutch, her energy requirements during incubation are great.

Part of the female's increased energy demand is met by the male, who feeds her regularly throughout the day. Sometimes he disappears into the cavity with food, and other times he softly sings *tuee, tuee* just outside the nest hole, prompting the female to emerge and take the food item outside. In Pielou's study, bouts of continuous incubation ranged in length from 6 to 52 minutes, averaging about half an hour.

During the incubation period, the contribution of food by the male is necessary for the development of the eggs. Although the female normally comes off the clutch for short periods to drink, bathe, and search for food on her own, she would not be able to incubate the eggs adequately if she did not have food brought to her by her mate. Such feeding allows the female to remain incubating for a larger portion of the day. Just before leaving the nest each time, the female carefully pulls a cover of hair and fibers over the eggs. This probably functions both to reduce the cooling rate of the eggs and to conceal them from potential nest predators.

When the female does leave her incubation duties, she forages near the male and usually high in the canopy. When returning to the nest, often from a distance of 50 to 100 meters, she flies directly and silently to perch perhaps 5 to 10 meters from the cavity. There she sits absolutely still and quiet for several minutes, then darts silently for the entrance hole. This sequence seems to be adaptive behavior to minimize the chances of the female giving away the location of the cavity to nest predators.

Pielou termed the time a female was sitting on her eggs the attentive period and the time she was away from the nest the inattentive period. The average duration of the attentive period was 25.8 minutes and the inattentive period 8.9 minutes. Pielou could find no relation between the length of these periods and any particular time of day.

Twice incubating females made a hissing sound as Pielou was investigating a nest cavity. I have experienced similar hissing in my studies of incubating Carolina Chickadees, and the vocalization has also been documented in several European titmice. Could such behavior have evolved to mimic the sound uttered by a snake? Would such a hiss deter an egg-hunting predator such as a red squirrel? Those with red squirrels in their backyards might tape a hissing noise, then play it back through a small remote speaker inside a cavity when a squirrel approaches. I wonder if titmice hiss in Ireland, a land with no snakes?

Pielou determined that the length of the incubation period for four nests averaged thirteen days and three hours. The eggs in a given nest hatched within ten to eighteen hours of each other. The female carried the eggshells a considerable distance from the nest, but Pielou was not able to determine whether they were eaten by the female or dropped. It might be adaptive for the female to eat the shells, as their calcium content would replenish that used in constructing the shells.

Though spotted on the outside, titmouse eggs are uniformly white on the inner surface, as are the eggshells of most birds. Even though titmice nest in cavities in rather low light intensities, removing the shells might make the nests less noticeable to visually hunting predators. Studies of open-nesting birds have shown that by removing the shells, parents reduce the ability of predators to find and consume the just-hatched nestlings.

After the eggs have hatched, the female spends a considerable part of the first day or two brooding the nestlings. During this period, the male brings food for both the female and the young.

In European titmice, during the nestlings' fifth to seventh days, the parents bring many more spiders as food than when the nestlings are either younger or older. This variation cannot be due to a temporary flush of spiders, because it has been found in both early- and late-breeding pairs. The reason for this is not known; perhaps spiders contain a particular nutrient required in greater amounts during a brief phase of nestling development.

The nestlings leave the nest at sixteen or seventeen days old, having turned from naked, blind, cold-blooded hatchlings into fully feathered, sharp-eyed, warm-blooded juveniles. Such rapid growth requires continual feeding by both parents sixteen to eighteen hours a day. During one glorious day in May, I sat in a lawn chair under a titmouse nest cavity and tallied the parents' rate of food delivery. Every three or four minutes all day long, the birds disappeared into the hole carrying billfuls of food.

Pielou found that when the nestlings were one day old, the female parent fed them about three times per hour and the male about five and a half times per hour. These rates gradually increased through the nestling period until, at day twelve, the female fed them eight times per hour and the male nine and a half times. These rates would need to be divided by the number of nestlings to determine feeding rates per individual young bird. By day twelve, the male was no longer feeding the female, and she was brooding the nestlings only during cold weather and at night.

After the nestlings are several days old, the parents carry out of the nest cavity what are called fecal sacs, mucus-covered packages of feces that the parents grasp with their bills while they are being excreted by the nestlings.

The parents carry such sacs several dozen meters from the hole and drop them in the woods. Such behavior is thought to improve nest sanitation and to remove visual and olfactory cues that might be useful to nest predators. But fecal sac carrying starts only after several days of nestling life. Very young nestlings also excrete fecal sacs, but instead of removing them, the parents eat them.

The fecal sacs of very young nestlings contain quite a bit of energy that has passed through the nestlings' digestive tract without being assimilated across the gut lining. The digestive efficiency of older nestlings improves to the point where very little energy passes out of their guts undigested. This suggests that the parents eat the feces of very young nestlings in order to benefit from the energy and nutrients that were not utilized by the nestlings. Sac consumption would have no benefit as the nestlings age, so the habit is abandoned.

As the nestlings age past twelve or thirteen days, they become restless, climbing over one another and exercising their wings. All through the nestling period and on into the early fledgling period, young birds often are fed by elder brothers or sisters in addition to their parents. In one study, the helper at the nest was a previous year's offspring of the female but was unrelated to the male of the breeding pair. In another case, the helper was the previous year's offspring of the same breeding pair.

As genetic analyses have not yet been done on titmice, it is not known whether the helper could actually be the father of some of the nestlings. It has been shown in some tropical cooperatively breeding species, however, that the helpers sometimes are genetic parents of some of the nestlings they are helping to raise.

This young Tufted Titmouse is within minutes of fledging, or flying for the first time. Pielou observed fledging to occur during both morning and evening. There is no evidence that the young birds are pushed or enticed from the nest by their parents. They just seem to leave when they are ready to go, though it is possible that they could sometimes get a boost from their brothers and sisters behind them in the nest. They will leave several days earlier than normal if the nest is disturbed. This early-departure response seems highly adaptive, as it would get them away from whatever disturbed the nest, perhaps some predator. Researchers must be very careful not to band nestlings older than about eleven days of age so as not to provoke such premature departure.

Pielou was able to watch the process of fledging in one nest. The first indication that fledging was imminent was that the young birds repeatedly came to the cavity entrance and looked out. At 9:15 A.M., three young flew from the cavity in rapid order, landing in some shrubbery about fifteen meters away. The two remaining nestlings flew to the same patch of vegetation at 10:35 A.M. During the fledging event, both parents remained in the vicinity, flying agitatedly and continually rendering a *tsick-a-de-dee* vocalization.

Over the next hour, the family slowly progressed about twenty-five meters through the trees, with the young ones following their parents and giving *seep-seep* calls. All five fledglings and their parents spent that night roosting in a thicket not far from the nest cavity.

For the first few days after fledging, young birds are quite immobile, perching in heavy cover close to the nest cavity but rapidly wing-quivering and giving the *see-see-see* vocalization at the approach of a parent carrying food. Gradually, over the next several weeks, they move with their parents about the family home range, practicing their flying skills and becoming acquainted with food and predators, knowledge that will serve them well as they prepare for autumn dispersal. Pielou saw the fledglings from one nest first feed themselves five days after leaving the cavity. By six weeks of age, the young birds were definitely foraging for themselves, and no begging was heard.

The pair's (particularly the male's) defense of the territory decreases noticeably during the nestling and fledgling stages of the reproductive period. For example, in contrast with almost daily observations of boundary disputes early in the breeding season, Pielou counted only one example of territorial defense during the nestling stage, that for one pair with day-old nestlings. Pielou attributed the decrease in territoriality to the male's intense new duties as provider of food for his family. Once the young have fledged, boundaries seem to break down altogether, with family parties continually trespassing on each other's ground. Whatever adaptive function territorial behavior serves, it is lost by the fledgling stage.

A titmouse nesting attempt can be unsuccessful, with no young fledging, for many reasons. Cold weather can force the female to abandon incubation. The cavity tree or snag can fall over, destroying the nest.

The eggs or nestlings can be taken by a predator as was the case with this nest. The cavity can be taken over by a house wren, a ferocious competitor for nest cavities. Titmice will renest if a nesting attempt is thwarted, but there are no records of a pair bringing off more than one set of fledglings in the same year.

5

Of Titmice and Men

Titmice enrich our lives. Our winter mornings are brightened as we hear an adult male giving the rallying call to gather the flock from their dispersed roost sites. The quiet elegance of their rather formal attire can be a welcome relief from the shameless flamboyance of male cardinals and goldfinches.

We also can admire their remarkable capacities. Imagine a 20-gram bird carrying on routinely in weather that requires us to don the entire contents of an L. L. Bean catalog. And even before the arrival of the first Red-winged Blackbird and the first Killdeer, the melodious *peter-peter-peter* from the high tree at the back of the garden is, during many years, absolutely the first sign that winter will not last forever.

Titmice are heavily affected by our activities. The birds evolved in continuous forest, particularly forest with mast-bearing trees. When European man arrived on the shores of North America, he found the world's greatest expanse of broad-leaved deciduous forest, and he has been cutting it down ever since. In 1875, virtually all of Ohio was forested. Now many counties have less than 10 percent of their acreage in trees, some less than 5 percent. The trees that remain are in island woodlots in a sea of grainfields.

How have the titmice coped with this massive destruction of their habitat? Paul Doherty and I have been studying this question within a 38,000-acre agricultural landscape in north-central Ohio. From banding titmice over several years, we know they are found at times in woodlots down to 4 or 5 acres in size, but not many individual birds persist in areas this small. These may be what are called sink habitats, small woodlots where titmice continually die without reproducing, only to be replaced by young birds dispersing in from source habitats—the larger woodlots and riverside forests.

We are also studying the possibility that titmice and other birds may combine several woodlots into one home range. Although individual woodlots may be too small to allow successful survival and reproduction, the aggregate area of two or three such small woodlands may suffice.

The issue may hinge on whether titmice are willing to cross the gaps between woodlots. There appears to be some upper limit to the width of field the birds will cross. The reluctance to cross large open spaces is probably related to predation risk. A titmouse caught in the open by a Cooper's Hawk is a dead titmouse, so there should be strong selection limiting the distance titmice cross. We hope to discover how close together woodlands should be left in order to promote gap crossing by woodland birds. Another issue is the quality of these woodlots. Large-scale spraying for gypsy moths and other forest pests has not only killed off nontarget insects used for food by titmice, but it has undoubtedly killed titmice directly as well.

The activities of humans can also be beneficial to titmice, however. The northward extension of the species' range has been credited to winter feeding. Some years ago, David Cimprich and I measured feather growth bars and showed that titmice wintering near bird feeders are in better nutritional condition than those without access to such supplementary food. In several studies of the Black-capped Chickadee, birds provided with extra food had a better chance of surviving the winter.

Humans also benefit titmice by providing them with artificial nesting cavities in the form of nestboxes and sometimes the furnishings with which to line their nests. This help is particularly important in areas where dead trees, known as snags, have been cut down either for firewood or simply because they are held to be unsightly. It is much better to leave a snag than to install a box.

The titmouse is a woodland thermometer, an indicator of woodland health. A woods with titmice will also have a healthy diversity of insects, a source of wildlife cover from the gales of winter, a stand of healthy mast-bearing trees, and snags to be used by many cavity-nesting species. It probably also has a spectacular carpet of spring wildflowers. All in all, any woodland attractive to titmice is also likely to be a restorative place for humans.

Selected References

Berner, T. O., and T. C. Grubb, Jr. 1985. An experimental analysis of mixed-species flocking in birds of deciduous woodland. *Ecology* 66:1229–36.

Braun, D., G. B. Kitto, and M. J. Braun. 1984. Molecular population genetics of tufted and black-crested forms of *Parus bicolor. Auk* 101:170–73.

Cimprich, D. A., and T. C. Grubb, Jr. 1994. Consequences for Carolina Chickadees of foraging with Tufted Titmice in winter. *Ecology* 75:1615–25.

Dixon, K. L. 1955. An ecological analysis of the interbreeding of crested titmice. *University of California Publications in Zoology* 54:125–205.

Dixon, K. L. 1990. Constancy of margins of the hybrid zone in titmice of the *Parus bicolor* complex in coastal Texas. *Auk* 107:184–87.

Ekman, J. 1989. Ecology of nonbreeding social systems of *Parus. Wilson Bulletin* 101:263–88.

Elder, W. H. 1985. Survivorship in the Tufted Titmouse. *Wilson Bulletin* 97:517–24.

Gill, F. B., D. H. Funk, and B. Silverin. 1989. Protein relationships among titmice (*Parus*). *Wilson Bulletin* 101:182–97.

Gill, F. B., and B. Slikas. 1992. Patterns of mitochondrial DNA divergence in North American crested titmice. *Condor* 94:20–28.

Grubb, T. C., Jr. 1975. Weather-dependent foraging behavior of some birds wintering in a deciduous woodland. *Condor* 77:175–82.

Grubb, T. C., Jr. 1994. Ptilochronology: A review and prospectus. *Current Ornithology* 12:89–114.

Grubb, T. C., Jr., and D. A. Cimprich. 1990. Supplementary food improves the nutritional condition of wintering woodland birds: Evidence from ptilochronology. *Ornis Scandinavica* 21:277–81.

Grubb, T. C., Jr., and V. V. Pravosudov. 1994. Tufted Titmouse (*Parus bicolor*). In *Birds of North America,* No. 86 (A. Poole and F. Gill, eds.). Philadelphia, The Academy of Natural Sciences.

Grubb, T. C., Jr., and V. V. Pravosudov. 1994. Toward a general theory of energy management in wintering birds. *Journal of Avian Biology* 25:255–60.

Hill, G. E. 1986. The function of distress calls given by Tufted Titmice (*Parus bicolor*): An experimental approach. *Animal Behaviour* 34:590–98.

Petit, D. R., L. J. Petit, and K. E. Petit. 1989. Winter caching behavior of deciduous woodland birds and adaptations for protection of stored food. *Condor* 91:766–76.

Pielou, W. P. 1957. A life-history study of the Tufted Titmouse, *Parus bicolor* Linnaeus. Ph.D. Dissertation, Michigan State University, East Lansing.

Schroeder, D. J., and R. H. Wiley. 1983. Communication with repertoires of song themes in Tufted Titmice. *Animal Behaviour* 31:1128–38.

Sherry, D. 1989. Food storing in the Paridae. *Wilson Bulletin* 101:289–304.

Sibley, C. G., and B. L. Monroe. 1990. Distribution and taxonomy of birds of the world. *Yale University Press,* New Haven, Connecticut.

Tarbell, A. T. 1983. A yearling helper with a Tufted Titmouse brood. *Journal of Field Ornithology* 54:89.

Waite, T. A., and T. C. Grubb, Jr. 1987. Dominance, foraging, and predation risk in the Tufted Titmouse. *Condor* 89:936–40.

Photo Credits

Page 1
Leonard Lee Rue III

Page 2
Steve Maslowski/
  Maslowski Photo (top)
Steven Bentsen
  (bottom)

Page 3
Steve Maslowski/
  Maslowski Photo (top)
H. Clarke/VIREO
  (bottom)

Page 4
Russell C. Hansen (top)
Jim Roetzel (bottom)

Page 5
Bill Duyck (top)
Jim Roetzel (bottom)

Page 6
Steve Maslowski/
  Maslowski Photo

Page 7
Leonard Lee Rue III
  (top)
Richard Day/Daybreak
  Imagery (middle)
Richard Day/Daybreak
  Imagery (bottom)

Page 8
Russell C. Hansen (top)
Leonard Lee Rue III
  (bottom)

Page 9
Richard Day/Daybreak
  Imagery

Page 10
Steve Maslowski/
  Maslowski Photo

Page 11
Steven Bentsen (top)
Richard Day/Daybreak
  Imagery (bottom)

Page 12
Russell C. Hansen

Page 13
Steven Bentsen

Page 14
Steve Maslowski/
  Maslowski Photo (top)
Jim Roetzel (middle)
Stephen Kirkpatrick
  (bottom)

Page 15
Steve Maslowski/
  Maslowski Photo (top)
Jim Roetzel (bottom)

Page 16
Jim Roetzel (top)
Steve Maslowski/
  Maslowski Photo
  (middle)
Gary W. Carter (bottom)

Page 17
Dave Dvorak, Jr. (top)
Dave Dvorak, Jr.
  (bottom)

Page 18
Gary W. Carter (top)
Jim Roetzel (bottom)

Page 19
Gary W. Carter

Page 20
Jim Roetzel

Page 21
Tom Evans (top)
Tom Vezo (middle)
Stephen Kirkpatrick
  (bottom)

Page 22
Leonard Lee Rue III

Page 23
Tom Vezo

Page 24
Tom Vezo (top)
Richard Day/Daybreak
  Imagery (bottom)

Page 25
Deborah Allen (top)
Gary W. Carter (bottom)

Page 26
Steve Maslowski/
  Maslowski Photo

Page 27
Steve Maslowski/
  Maslowski Photo

Page 28
Gary W. Carter (top)
Steve Maslowski/
  Maslowski Photo
  (bottom)

Page 29
Russell C. Hansen

Page 30
Richard Day/Daybreak
  Imagery (top)
Richard Day/Daybreak
  Imagery (middle)
Dave Dvorak, Jr.
  (bottom)

Page 31
Dave Dvorak, Jr.

Page 32
Steve Maslowski/
  Maslowski Photo (top)
Steve Maslowski/
  Maslowski Photo
  (bottom)

Page 33
Richard Day/Daybreak
  Imagery (top)
Steven Bentsen
  (bottom)

Page 34
Connie Toops (top)
Leonard Lee Rue III
  (bottom)

Page 35
Richard Day/Daybreak
  Imagery

Page 36
Dave Dvorak, Jr. (top)
Bob de Lange /VIREO
  (bottom)

Page 37
Richard Day/Daybreak
  Imagery (top)
Jim Roetzel (bottom)

Page 38
Richard Day/Daybreak
  Imagery (top)
Connie Toops (bottom)

Page 39
Jim Roetzel (top)
Richard Day/Daybreak
  Imagery (bottom)

Page 40
Tom Vezo (top)
V. Hasselblad/VIREO
  (bottom)

Page 41
Given Photography
  (top)
Tom Vezo (bottom)

Page 42
Gary W. Carter (top)
Steve Maslowski/
  Maslowski Photo
  (bottom)

Page 43
Dave Dvorak, Jr.(top)
Dave Dvorak, Jr.
 (middle)
Tom Vezo (bottom)

Page 44
Jim Roetzel (top)
Richard Day/Daybreak
 Imagery (bottom)

Page 45
Leonard Lee Rue III

Page 46
Steve Maslowski/
 Maslowski Photo (top)
Connie Toops (bottom)

Page 47
Richard Day/Daybreak
 Imagery (top)
Given Photography
 (bottom)

Page 48
Connie Toops (top)
Tom Vezo (bottom)

Page 49
Steve Maslowski/
 Maslowski Photo (top)
Leonard Lee Rue III
 (bottom)

Page 50
Steve Maslowski/
 Maslowski Photo

Page 51
Steve Maslowski/
 Maslowski Photo (top)
Gary W. Carter (bottom)

Page 52
Tom Vezo

Page 53
Russell C. Hansen

Page 54
Tom Vezo

Page 55
Jim Roetzel (top)
Gary W. Carter (bottom)

Page 56
Deborah Allen

Page 57
Deborah Allen

Page 58
Connie Toops

Page 59
Gary W. Carter (top)
Gary W. Carter (bottom)

Page 60
Leonard Lee Rue III
 (top)
Connie Toops (bottom)

Page 61
Bill Duyck (top)
Stephen Kirkpatrick
 (bottom)

Page 62
Steve Maslowski/
 Maslowski Photo (top)
Leonard Lee Rue III
 (bottom)

Page 63
Jim Roetzel (top)
Richard Day/ Daybreak
 Imagery (bottom)

Page 64
Bill Duyck (top)
Bill Duyck (bottom)

Page 65
Tom Evans (top)
John Serrao (bottom)

Page 66
Bill Duyck (top)
Leonard Lee Rue III
 (bottom)

Page 67
Bill Duyck

Page 68
Bill Duyck (top)
Bill Duyck (bottom)

Page 69
Bill Duyck (top)
Bill Duyck (bottom)

Page 70
Connie Toops

Page 71
Bill Duyck (top)
Bill Duyck (middle)
Bill Duyck (bottom)

Page 72
Bill Duyck

Page 73
Connie Toops (top)
Jim Roetzel (bottom)

Page 74
Richard Day/Daybreak
 Imagery

Page 75
Jim Roetzel

Page 76
Richard Day/Daybreak
 Imagery (top)
Tom Vezo (bottom)

Page 77
Given Photography

Page 78
Dave Dvorak, Jr.

Page 79
Richard Day/Daybreak
 Imagery

Page 80
Steve Maslowski/
 Maslowski Photo

About the Author

Thomas C. Grubb, Jr. is a professor in the Department of Zoology at The Ohio State University. He served for two years on the faculty of Rutgers University, where he began studying the winter biology of woodland birds before moving on the The Ohio State University in 1973. In subsequent years, he has continued his research on "winter birds" and recently developed "ptilochronology", a new method for monitoring the nutritional condition of free-ranging birds. He is the author of *Beyond Birding: Field Projects for Inquisitive Birders,* a text that introduces the scientific method to students and amateur birders. He lives near Columbus, Ohio.

Index